Tweenies™

bakers, builders and busy people

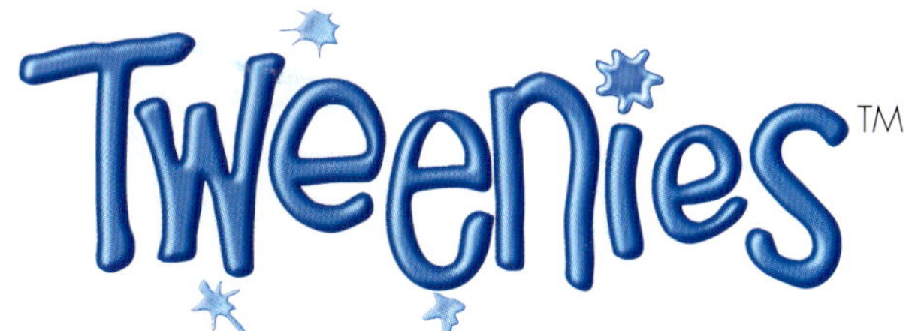

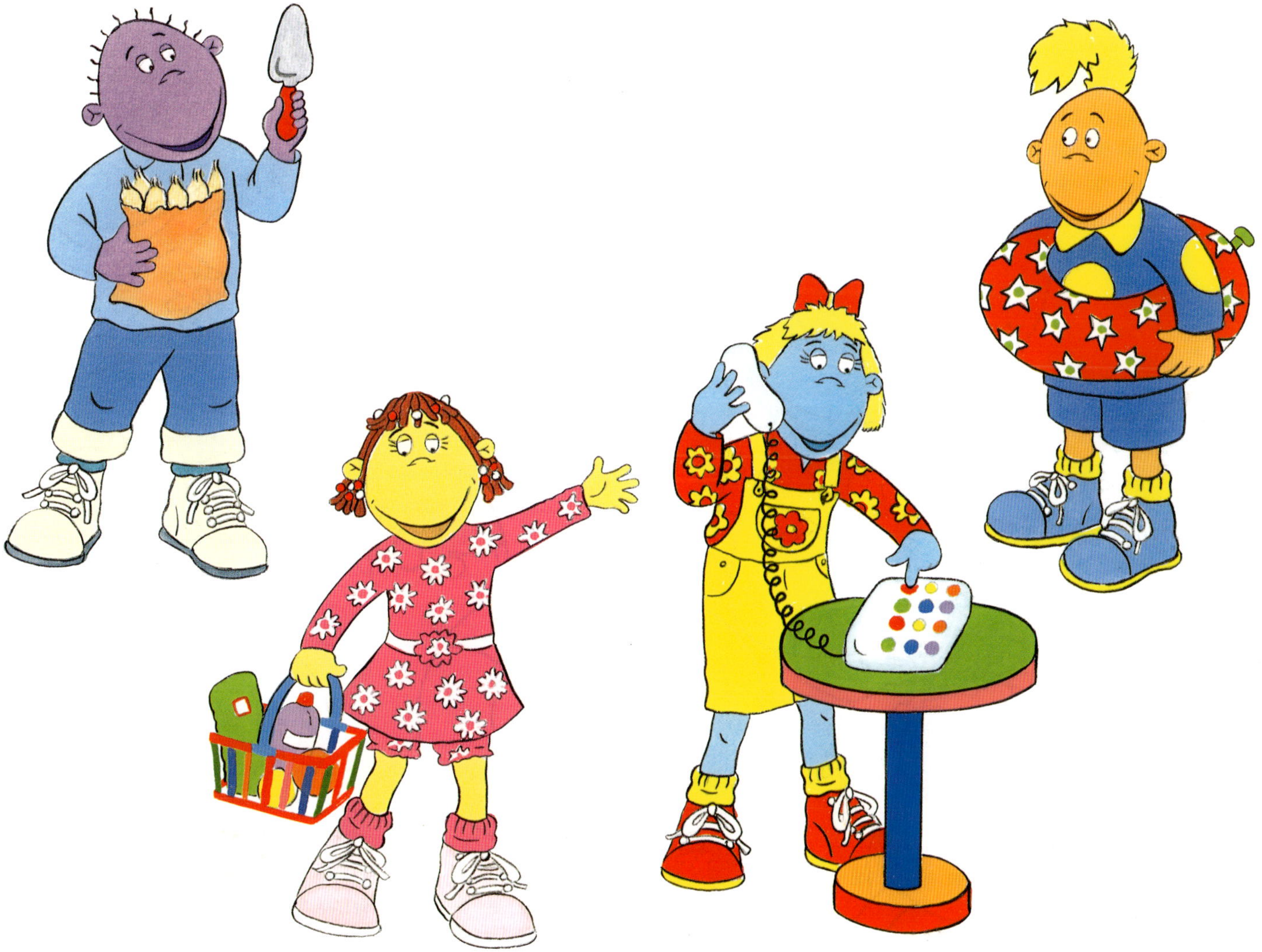

look book

BBC

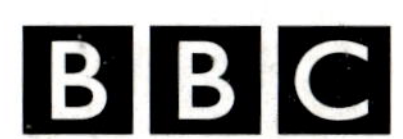

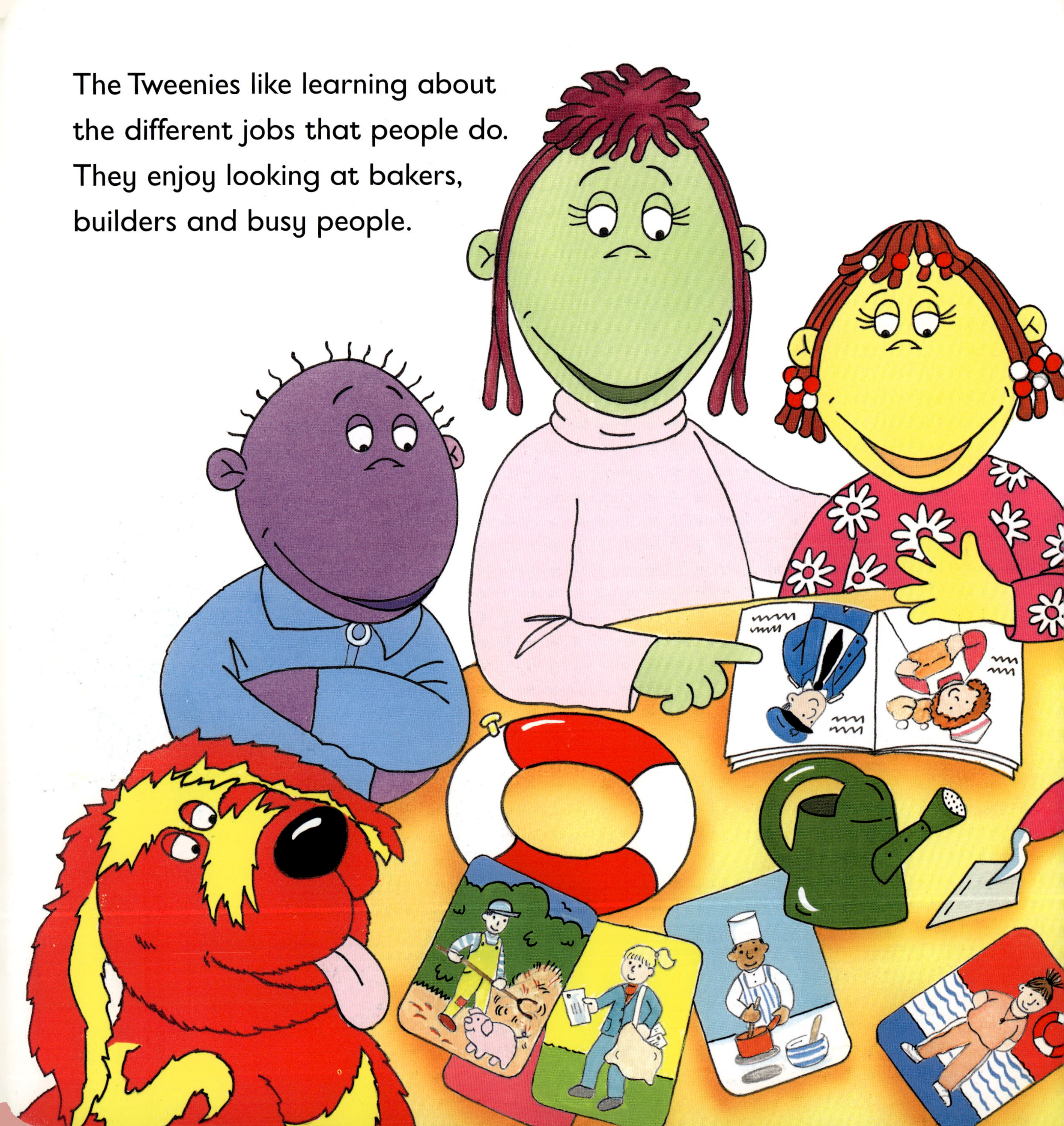

The Tweenies like learning about
the different jobs that people do.
They enjoy looking at bakers,
builders and busy people.

telly time

Jake tells Max that he wants to find out more about what jobs people do at a sports centre. Max shows him a video all about it.

Word time

- dance teacher
- nursery nurse
- gym instructor
- lifeguard
- tennis coach
- waiter

Max and Jake are visiting the local sports centre. They have watched some people learning how to play tennis and now they stop to watch a swimming lesson.
changing rooms
learning pool
arm bands

life belt
oar
ladder
swimming lane
teacher
goggles
rubber ring
lifeguard
float

telly time

Fizz likes going into town
and looking at all the shops.
The people who work there
do lots of different jobs.
Judy shows Fizz a video
about a town centre.

TOWN BANK
Maria's Bakery
Mini market
Word time
cashier
baker
postwoman
computer programmer
greengrocer
delivery man

Judy and Fizz go to see the mini market where lots of different foods are on sale. The shopkeeper sells milk, eggs, cheese, cereals, juice and newspapers.

store room
shelves
book rack

Make your own shop

When Fizz gets back to the other Tweenies, she tells Jake all about the shop. They decide to make a model of one.

You will need:

apron 

a medium-sized cardboard box 

a small cardboard box 

paints and brushes 

glue or sticky tape 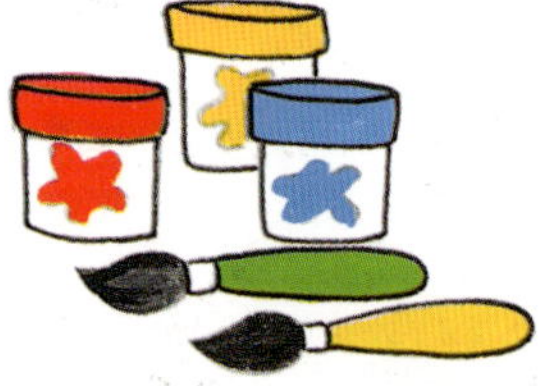

modelling clay

round-ended scissors 

1) Ask an adult to help you cut off the top and front of the medium-sized box.

2) Paint a shop scene inside
the box.

3) Paint the small box so it looks
like a shop counter. When it's dry,
glue or stick it in your model.

4) Shape different kinds of food
from the modelling clay. Display
them on your counter.

5) Make a clay model of a
shopkeeper and put it behind
the counter.

Milo tells Judy that when he gets a job, he wants to work outdoors. Judy shows him a video about different jobs outdoors.

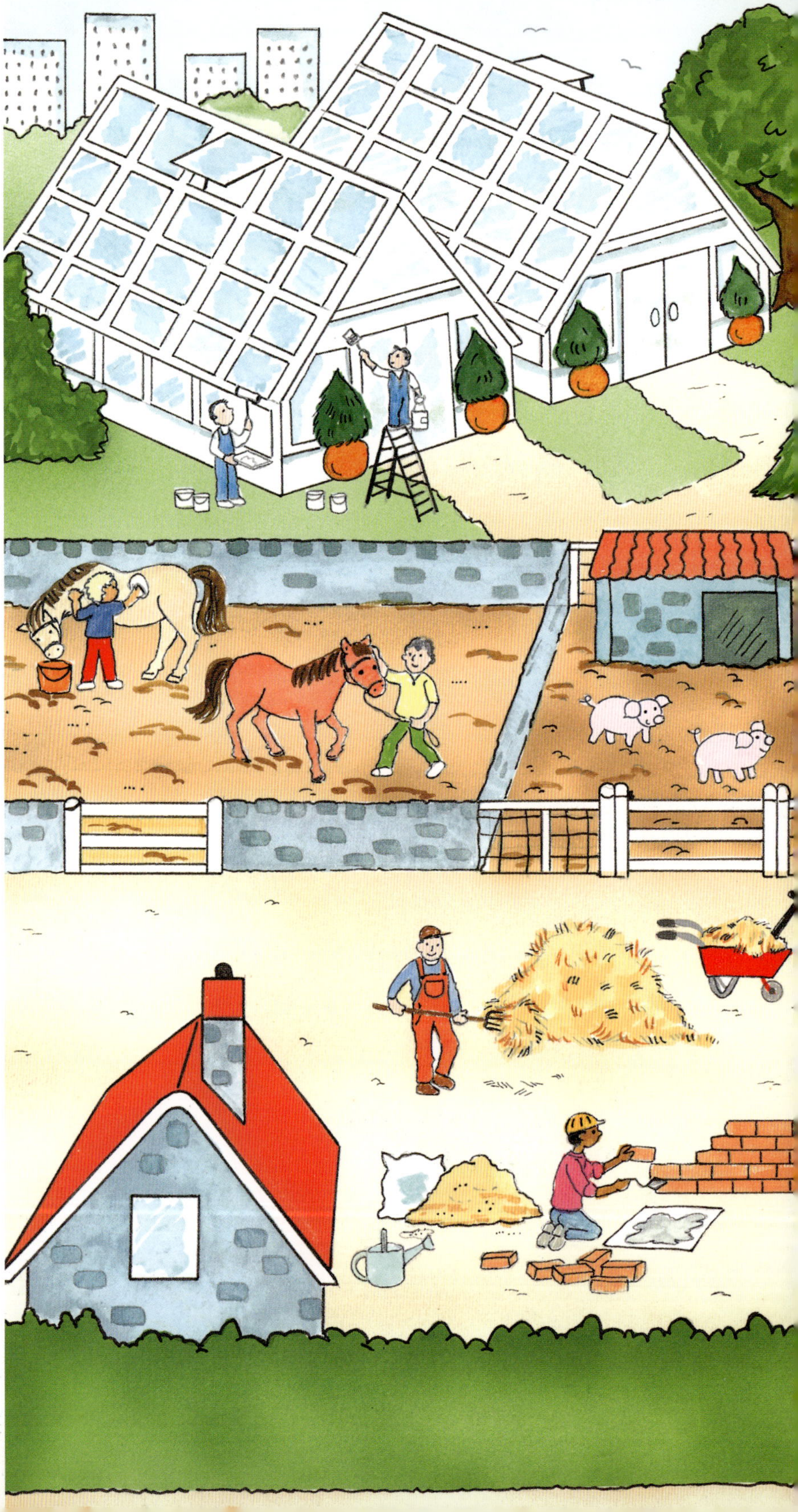

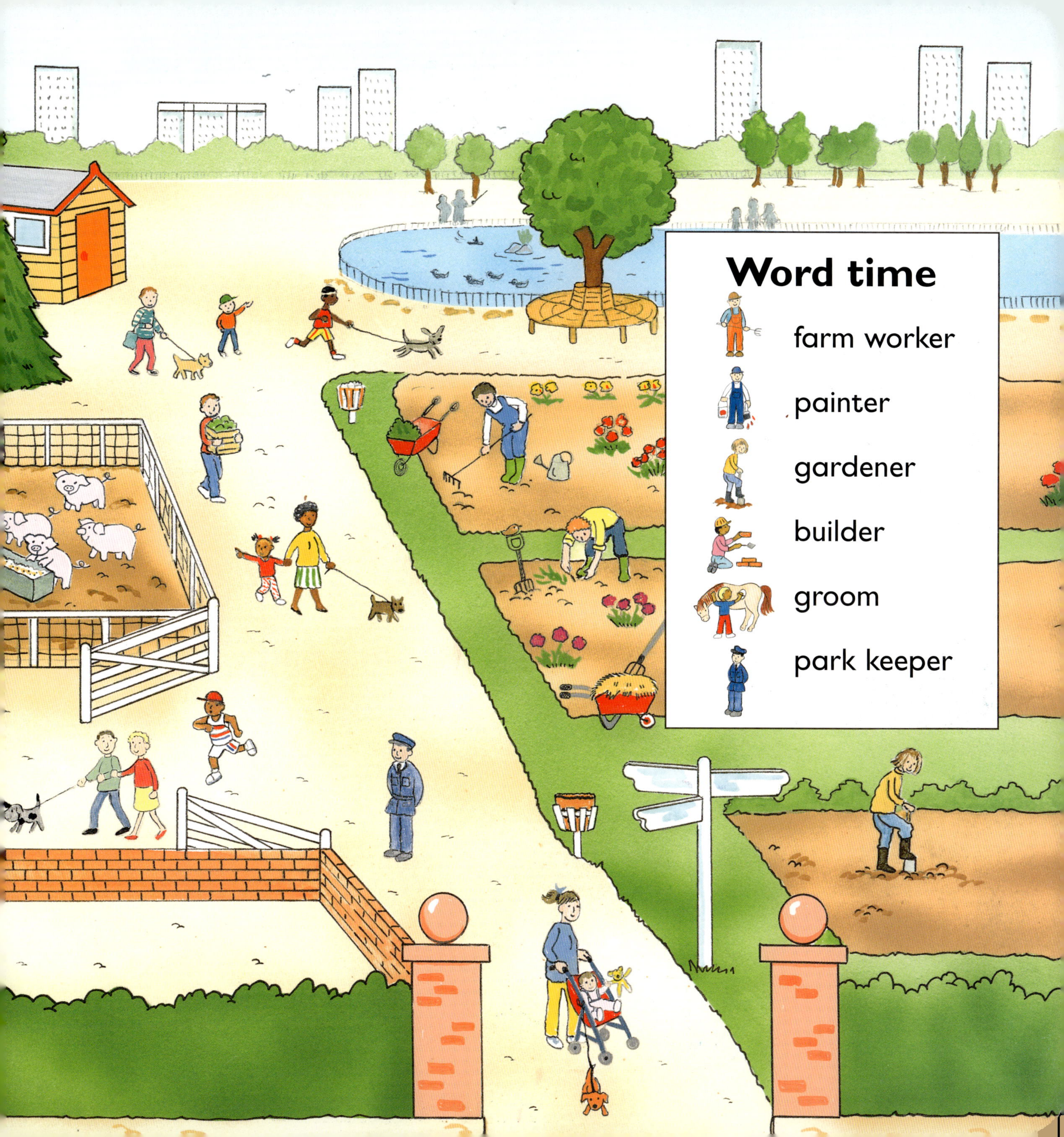
Word time
farm worker
painter
gardener
builder
groom
park keeper

Judy takes Milo to visit a park.
Milo decides that he would like to
be a gardener in a park when he
grows up. There are so many
things to do.

tractor driver
litter collector
flower bed
rake

telly time

Bella thinks that offices are exciting places to work, because there are so many different jobs to do. Max shows her a video all about offices.

Word time
security guard
courier
window
cleaner
snack seller
office assistant
chef

Max takes Bella to visit an office, where they can see people working, talking on the telephone, using computers and meeting.
manager
receptionist
telephonist
computer
desk
filing cabinet

delivery man
water cooler
printer
fax machine
post tray
sandwich seller

Make your own telephone

When Bella gets back to the other Tweenies, Milo helps her make a model of a telephone.

You will need:-

apron

one large and one small cardboard box

pencil

round-ended scissors

paints and brushes

sticky tape

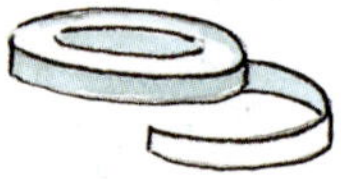

strips of crêpe paper

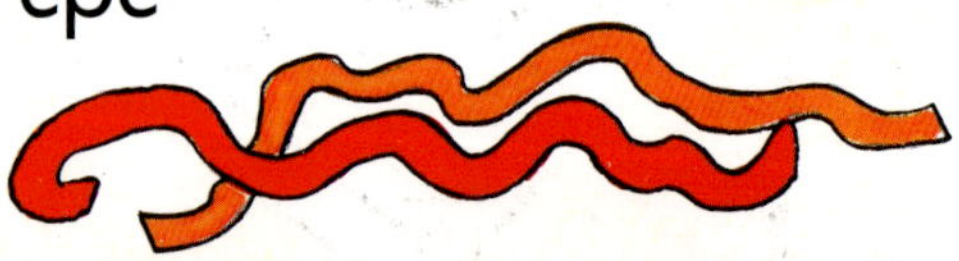

1) Paint your cardboard boxes.

2) When the bigger box is dry, draw circles where the buttons should be.

3) Take the smaller box and draw two circles. One circle goes against your ear and the other is for your mouth.

4) Stick one end of a crêpe paper strip to one box, and the other end to the other box. You're ready to make a phone call!

The Tweenies have had a busy time learning about
bakers, builders and busy people. They have learned
about the different jobs that people do, and have
made their own shops and telephones.